Mighty Mission Machines

From Rockets to Rovers

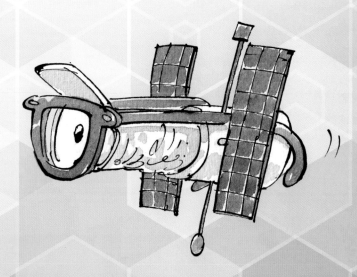

Dave Williams, MD, and Loredana Cunti
art by Theo Krynauw

annick press
toronto + berkeley

Contents

Welcome from Dr. Dave

Exploration is all about teams and machines.
Success takes creativity, science, and technology.

Dr. Dave Williams

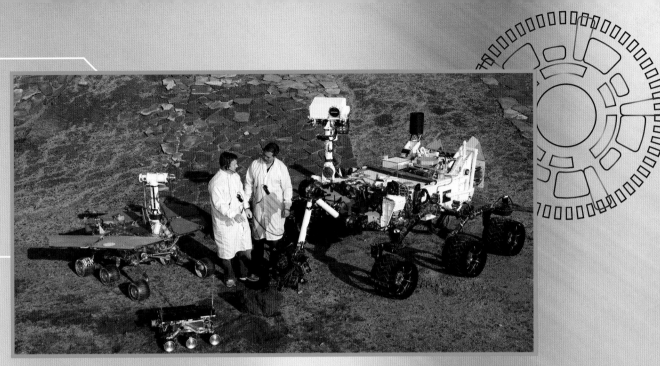

NASA engineers with test models of three different Mars rovers: *Sojourner*, *MER*, and *Curiosity*

Every day, thousands of people around the world—scientists, engineers, mathematicians, technicians, and others—work hard to support space programs and exploration. But even with all of that support, there are certain things you just can't do without the right equipment. In this book, we'll explore the rockets, rovers, robots, computers, and gadgets that help astronauts travel, live, and work in space.

—Dr. Dave

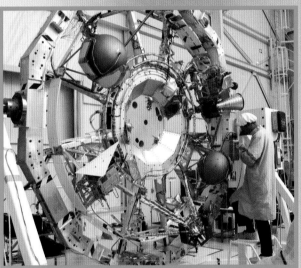

Mars Exploration Rover 1 in the lab

Astronaut Tracy Caldwell Dyson gets help suiting up for launch.

Mighty Machines

Astronauts have a super-cool job—exploring outer space. But they can't do it on their own. It's dangerous for humans in space, and the moons and planets we want to visit are farther away than we can even imagine. Without a lot of mighty machines, amazing technology, and powerful equipment—along with a few basic tools, like good old hammers and wrenches—space missions would never get off the ground.

A view of Earth from Space Shuttle *Columbia*

How Far Is Far?

The farthest humans have traveled in outer space is to the Moon. The Moon is 386,242 kilometers (240,000 miles) from Earth—that's like walking around the entire planet 10 times. Since the average human walks at a pace of 5 kilometers (3.1 miles) per hour, a stroll isn't going to get you there. In fact, not even an airplane can help! When it comes to getting to outer space, a rocket is your new best friend.

Outer space is far! My first mission was on the Space Shuttle Columbia. We traveled 10 million kilometers (6.214 million miles), orbiting as high as 274 kilometers (170 miles) above Earth.

Danger Zone!

Imagine trying to live where there is no air to breathe and the temperature outside can be as hot as 121°C (250°F) or as cold as –157°C (–250°F). Oh, and did we mention the flying meteors, stellar explosions, and cosmic radiation? Well, that's space—and that's why astronauts must be protected to survive. Spacecraft, space suits, and planetary rovers all get the job done.

Astronaut Peggy Whitson on a space walk

Here We Come!

Where *Exactly* Is Space?

Ready to lift off? Great! But where exactly are you lifting off *to*?
What do we mean when we talk about space?

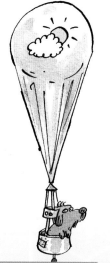

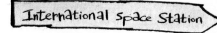 **547 kilometers**
340 miles

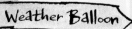 **400 kilometers**
249 miles

The Kármán Line

There's no actual border marking entry to outer space, but international space treaties use the Kármán line, at an altitude of 100 kilometers (62 miles) above sea level, as its start. Since an average 10-year-old can only jump about 25 centimeters (10 inches) off the ground, and most airplanes can only fly about 10.6 kilometers (6.6 miles) high, getting to outer space isn't easy. But it's not only about going up. Getting to space means getting *through* Earth's atmosphere.

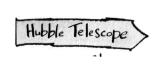 **100 kilometers**
62 miles

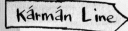 **40 kilometers**
25 miles

 10.6 kilometers
6.6 miles

 **Ground level**

6

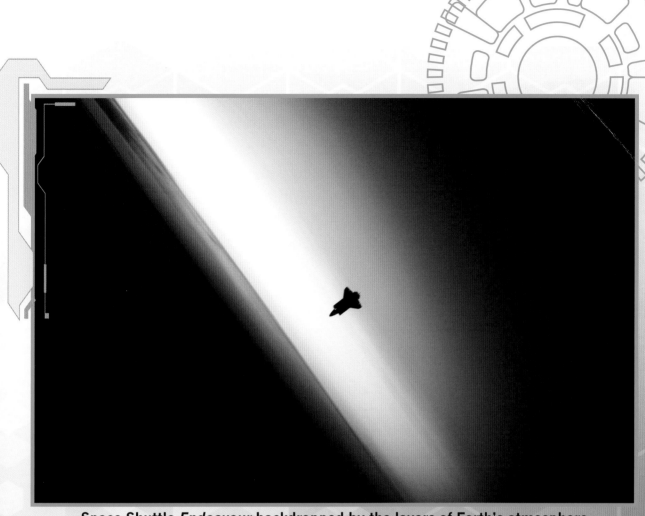

Space Shuttle *Endeavour* backdropped by the layers of Earth's atmosphere

Outta My Way, Atmosphere

The atmosphere is a layer of gases that surrounds Earth and is kept in place by the force of gravity. It warms the surface of the planet, reduces temperature swings between night and day, and absorbs the sun's ultra-violet radiation. That's all good news for the life-forms that call Earth home, but it's not so great when it comes to space travel. That's because astronauts need a machine that can fly fast enough to overcome gravity, push through the atmosphere, and get to orbit. Flying at almost 8 kilometers (5 miles) per second, rocket engines and spacecraft come in handy.

All Aboard!

A spacecraft is one incredible vehicle! In it, an astronaut can travel to outer space, orbit Earth, go to the Moon, or, in the future, visit other planets. Some, like the *Soyuz*, look like a capsule. Others, like the space shuttle, resemble an airplane. Whatever they look like, they have to be strong, but also light enough to fly fast and far. And they all have some basic parts in common.

BASIC STRUCTURE:
Spacecraft carrying humans have a flight deck with all the equipment necessary to navigate, communicate, and operate the onboard systems. Spacecraft are usually small, so everyone shares a living room, bathroom, and sleeping area.

Crunch Crunch Crunch

The Boeing 777 airplane engine produces a lot of thrust. It would take at least 75 of these engines to get the Space Shuttle to lift off.

The *Soyuz* capsule attached to its rocket

HEAT SHIELD:
As a spacecraft moves through Earth's atmosphere, the friction created generates a lot of heat. Without the heat shield, the spacecraft would burn up.

MAIN ENGINES:
No main engines, no liftoff. Some spacecraft can have as many as 27 engines to get their cargo into space.

FUEL TANKS:
All engines need fuel. Some spacecraft have fuel tanks just like the gas tank in a car. Others use booster rockets with the fuel stored inside.

POWER SUPPLY:
The International Space Station (ISS) uses as much power as 55 houses. Spacecraft use less.

PAYLOAD:
Payload is astronaut-speak for *cargo*. A spacecraft's payload bay might hold machines or equipment needed for the mission, scientific instruments or experiments, or supplies.

THRUSTERS:
Thrusters are small rocket engines that a spacecraft needs to move around in space, dock with another spacecraft, or come back to Earth.

Space Shuttle *Discovery* launches

Humans in Space

Spacecraft may seem like something from the future, but they aren't new technology at all. Starting in the 1960s, missions such as Vostok, Mercury, Gemini, and Apollo have been taking astronauts faster and farther into space.

Firsts in the Frontier

1961

FIRST MAN IN SPACE: Russian cosmonaut Yuri Gagarin on *Vostok 1*. The spacecraft's controls were automated just in case the spaceflight caused Gagarin to act a little strange. NASA astronaut Alan Shepard became the second person, and the first American, to travel into space.

1962

FIRST AMERICAN TO ORBIT EARTH: John Glenn circled Earth 3 times in 4 hours and 56 minutes.

1963

FIRST WOMAN IN SPACE: Valentina Tereshkova, *Vostok 6*. She spent three days alone in space.

A *cosmonaut* is a Russian astronaut. A *taikonaut* is a Chinese astronaut.

The first space shuttle was named *Enterprise* in response to letters from *Star Trek* fans. It was never designed to go to space. It had no engines or heat shield and was used only for landing tests.

1969

FIRST MOON LANDING: Neil Armstrong (left) became the first man to walk on the Moon, followed by Buzz Aldrin (right), both from *Apollo 11*. Armstrong also spoke the first words from the surface of the Moon: "That's one small step for man, one giant leap for mankind."

1965

FIRST SPACE WALKS: Alexei Leonov took a 10-minute stroll while attached by a cable to the outside of *Voskhod 2*, and Ed White (above) tested a special maneuvering unit while outside his Gemini spacecraft.

The first clear image from the surface of Mars, taken by *Viking 1*

1976

FIRST MARS LANDING: With no humans on board, *Viking 1* was a space probe controlled by scientists back on Earth. It transmitted the first pictures from the surface of the red planet.

Click

Meet Your Spacecraft

Over the years of space exploration, many types of spacecraft have been designed and built for different missions.

Artist's concept of *Voyager 2*

SPACESHIP: Carries humans. Example: *Soyuz*, which carries people and supplies to the International Space Station and around Earth.

INTERPLANETARY SPACECRAFT: Can reach other moons and planets in the solar system. Example: *Voyager 2*, which sent back the first close-up images of Neptune in 1989.

***Soyuz* prepares to launch.**

A worker sews insulation on the *Huygens* space probe before launch.

INTERSTELLAR SPACECRAFT OR SPACE PROBES: Can travel beyond our solar system to interstellar space. Example: *Voyager 1*, which left our solar system in 1992 to become the farthest human-made object from Earth.

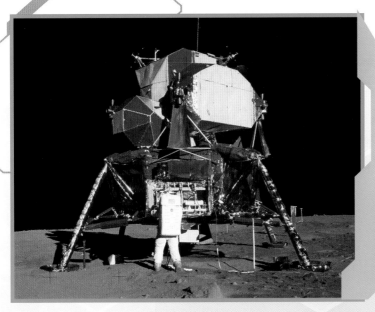

The "Eagle"

LANDER: Can land on the Moon or a planet. Example: the *Apollo 11* lunar module spacecraft, nicknamed "Eagle," which took the first humans to the Moon in 1969.

Mariner 9

ORBITER: Can achieve orbit around a planet. Example: *Mariner 9*, which, in 1971, became the first spacecraft to orbit Mars.

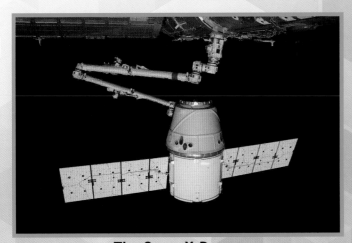

The SpaceX *Dragon*

What's in a Name?

NASA named its space shuttle spacecraft after famous exploration sailing ships: *Columbia, Challenger, Discovery, Atlantis, Endeavour*. Today, the Russian rocket and spacecraft shuttling astronauts from Earth to the ISS is called *Soyuz* (so-yooz), meaning "union." SpaceX, an aerospace company, calls its capsule *Dragon*.

Soy-What?

Over the years, different spacecraft have carried astronauts into space. Today, they travel on the *Soyuz*. This spacecraft launches on top of a *Soyuz* rocket and lifts off from the Baikonur Cosmodrome in Kazakhstan.

Lift Off!

With all the exhaust burning out of the bottom of the rockets, no wonder the *Soyuz* lifts off far away from anyone or anything that can get hurt. After the launch, the capsule and the rocket separate. The rocket returns to Earth while the capsule keeps going—and fast! It takes only nine minutes to reach space!

The *Soyuz* launches.

Cosmonaut Fyodor Yurchikhin and astronaut Jack Fischer in front of the *Soyuz*

What happens if an astronaut needs to get home from the space station? For every three crew members on the ISS, there is always at least one Soyuz (which has three seats) attached to the station.

14

Heavy Lifting

The space shuttle weighs over 1.8 million kilograms (4 million pounds) at liftoff. That's as heavy as four Airbus Airplanes! How can an engine lift that *and* get it going fast enough to escape that incredible force we call gravity? Thrust! To get to space, the thrust—or force—provided by the rocket engines has to be greater than the weight of the spacecraft. With enough thrust, you can make anything fly.

The space shuttle rocket engines consume so much liquid fuel that they would drain a family swimming pool filled with it every 25 seconds.

The base of the *Soyuz* rocket boosters

T-minus 10-9-8...

Soyuz blasts off into space.

Rev Those Engines

Rockets? Check. Fuel? Check. Astronauts? Check. You're ready to go. It's time to rev those engines and lift off!

And Now, On Stage . . .

Rockets use a complex computer system to ensure that they go the right way and get to space. But the first step is to get off the ground. Rockets work in stages, each with its own engines and fuel. When the fuel runs out, the part of the rocket that isn't needed anymore falls away. (It either burns up in the atmosphere or falls into uninhabited areas on land or in the ocean, where it can't hurt anyone.) The rocket is now lighter, and the next engine stage can do its job to propel the rocket, the spacecraft, and the astronauts farther.

After only eight and a half minutes—or less time than it takes to eat a sandwich—the engines shut down as the last of the fuel is consumed. The spacecraft travels on, covering 8 kilometers (5 miles) a second. In other words—fast!

The rocket and engine from Space Shuttle *Atlantis* work to launch the spacecraft through the clouds.

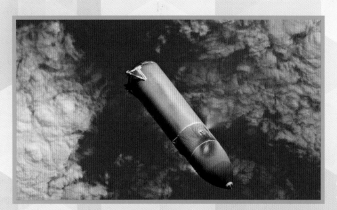

Space Shuttle *Discovery's* external fuel tank falls back toward Earth.

H-H-H-H-OOOOOOLD-ONNN!

Achieving Orbit

All of this power has to get the rocket moving fast enough to get into "orbit"—space-speak for circling really fast around and around Earth. In order to stay in orbit, spacecraft have to be traveling at an astonishing 28,163 kilometers (17,500 miles) per hour.

Apollo **spacecraft in orbit**

Riding on a space shuttle attached to solid rocket boosters is like riding in a pickup truck driving really fast on a bumpy dirt road. Everything is shaking and vibrating!

Home Away from Home

A Space Hotel

The ultimate "home away from home" is orbiting Earth right now. Since 2000, astronauts have been living on the ISS. Astronauts can call the ISS home for six months to one year, depending on the mission. At a height of 400 kilometers (249 miles) above Earth's surface, this research laboratory in the sky travels around our planet 32 times a day. That's like going to the Moon . . . and back!

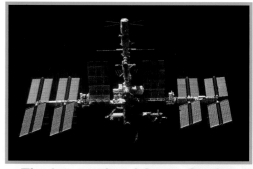

The International Space Station

Home on the ISS

Like your home, the ISS has heating and cooling, electrical power, communications, food and waste management, and water recycling. There are work areas, living areas, and even bedrooms. Doors, or hatches, connect small rooms (called "modules") where astronauts do different jobs and activities.

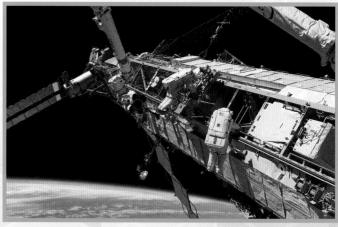

Dr. Dave on a space walk outside the ISS

Not for Sale

The most expensive house in the world is reportedly in India, valued at a whopping $1 billion. But that's planetary peanuts compared to the ISS. Over the years, 16 countries have worked together on the ISS, sending different missions with astronauts and supplies to complete the work. The result? The most expensive object ever built, at a cost of about $150 billion.

Astronaut Scott Kelly tweeted this photo of his bedroom aboard the ISS.

The ISS is the third-brightest object in the night sky after the Moon and Venus. You can actually spot it with the naked eye. It looks like a fast-moving airplane.

WELCOME to the SPACE STATION

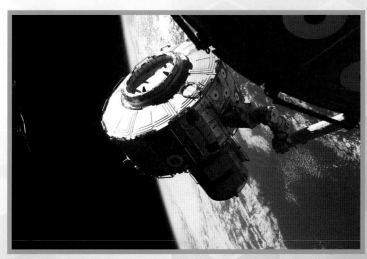
A robot arm moves the Quest Airlock into position on the ISS.

Airlocks for Astronauts

There are "airlocks," areas where astronauts prepare to move from inside, where there is air, to space, a vacuum where there is none. Without that transition, astronauts could not go outside. The ISS also features docking ports—like garages—where visiting spacecraft park to deliver astronauts and new supplies.

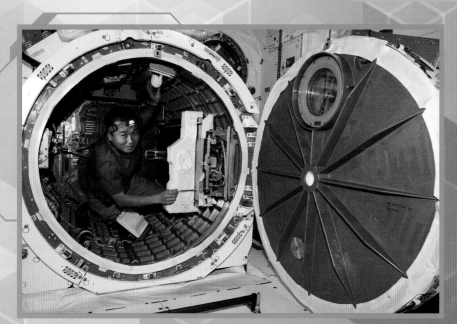
Astronaut Koichi Wakata works inside the Kibo airlock.

Has Anyone Seen a Plug?

Imagine not being able to plug in your tablet and recharge your battery. Just like you, astronauts living aboard the ISS need power to live comfortably, conduct their experiments, and operate the station. But there are no power stations in space! So how do they power up?

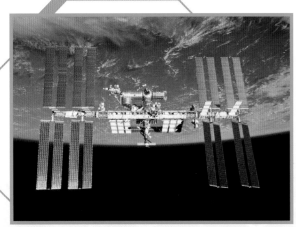

Solar panels capture the sun's energy to power the ISS.

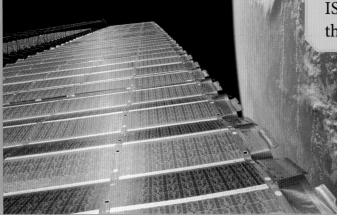

A close-up of a solar panel

Hello, Solar Power!

Being above the atmosphere has its advantages. First, there are no clouds. And second, traveling at that altitude and speed means the ISS goes around Earth every 90 minutes, which guarantees a sunrise every 45 minutes. That puts the space station's solar panels in a good position to capture solar energy! Once the solar panels produce electricity, it gets distributed through the ISS by wires called busses, powering all the lights and equipment.

Sunlight to Battery Life

But wait. All that circling of Earth means there's a *sunset* every 45 minutes, too, right? So what happens when the (sun)light goes out? To keep the amount of energy constant, the space station uses batteries that are recharged by the solar panels when in direct sunlight.

Astronaut Peggy Whitson in the Destiny Laboratory on board the ISS

Astronauts Kevin Ford and Robert Thirsk work the controls of the station's robotic arm.

Power on the ISS allows the crew to do almost everything you would do on Earth that needs electricity, including sending tweets, videos, and pictures from their laptops to people back home.

By the Numbers

The ISS is very well equipped for a home in outer space. On it, you will find:

* 2 bathrooms
* 3 exercise machines
* 6 crew members
* 16 solar panels
* 52 computers

Not bad, right? But don't look for a chair if you feel like taking a rest— there aren't any! Dr. Dave's advice is to just float!

Extraterrestrial Tents

The ISS is one type of space habitat, but around the world, space agencies are developing ways for astronauts to live and work on the Moon or another planet, like Mars.

Mars Mission

Space agencies dream of one day sending an astronaut to Mars. But to make that happen, a high-tech planetary habitat is needed. There are huge challenges when it comes to supporting life on Mars. There is no oxygen, temperatures are extreme, and radiation levels are high. A space habitat would require the same life-support systems as the ISS: oxygen supply, heating and cooling, power generation, water recycling, food, and waste management. Is it ever going to happen? Astronauts sure hope so.

Astronauts have never visited Mars—yet.

Are you imagining yourself as one of the first people on Mars? Get comfy! It will take you six months just to get there!

BEAM attached to the ISS

Beam Me Up!

The future is . . . inflatable! The next generation of space station modules and lunar or planetary habitats may be inflatable. Why? Because when the plan is to travel farther than ever before, carrying less weight is important. Inflatable habitats are already in use. To test one, NASA sent the Bigelow Expandable Activity Module (BEAM) to the ISS inside the SpaceX *Dragon* spacecraft in 2016. The ISS robotic arm was used to attach BEAM to the outside of the ISS. Then it was blown up like a bubble tent.

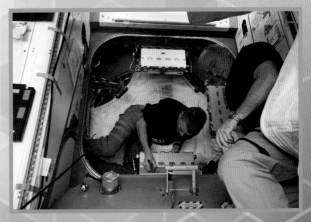

Astronauts Tim Peak and Jeff Williams prepare BEAM for inflation.

A Tough Job

While getting to outer space is a lot of work, it isn't an astronaut's main job. The real work of being an astronaut depends on the mission.

To-Do Today

Astronauts are busy! A typical workday in space could include:

* researching
* conducting science experiments
* maintaining the ISS
* checking spacecraft systems
* communicating with mission control
* taking pictures of Earth
* exercising
* eating
* cleaning

Astronaut Steve Swanson works on an experiment in the Destiny Laboratory of the ISS.

Brains in Space!

Dr. Dave's first mission was known as Neurolab or, as he likes to say, "My Brain in Space." The astronauts on that mission did tests to figure out how humans and other species adapt to being in space. Do we sleep the same way we do on Earth? How about sitting, standing, walking, and exercising? Can we tell which way is up? Astronauts want to know!

When astronauts aren't doing research, they're checking the onboard systems and performing routine maintenance tasks to keep everything in tip-top shape. They also have to keep their sleep station organized so stuff doesn't float away and get lost. It's true: even astronauts have to make their beds!

Fun facts: Most astronauts think "up" is always above their head, and some snore in space!

Astronaut Samantha Cristoforetti does maintenance work in the ISS Tranquility module.

Call in the Robots!

Humans may have visited the Moon, but robotic explorers have been to the Moon, Mars, Venus, Jupiter, and Saturn's largest moon, Titan—plus a few comets and asteroids! Robots are perfect for deep-space exploration: they don't eat, don't sleep, and can survive in hazardous conditions.

Robo Ready!

It can take an astronaut a few hours to get ready for a space walk. Luckily, robots are always ready to go. And when they are operated by remote control or through a computer, they can carry out extremely complex tasks. Some of these amazing machines— called "articulating robots"—are even built with the human body in mind. They have joints, like our knuckles and elbows, that allow them to hold parts and tools. Handy!

Onboard Buddy

The ISS has its very own onboard robot, named Robonaut. Designed to look like a person, it is sometimes used for simple space-walk activities. Something needs to be fixed? Send Robonaut! Inside the ISS, an astronaut can wear special gloves to perform an operation that Robonaut copies, and with a camera in Robonaut's head, an astronaut can see what Robonaut sees.

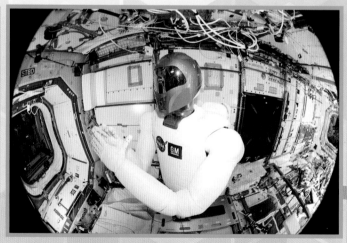

Robonaut following orders on the ISS

Canadarm

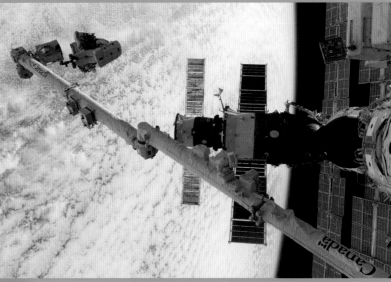

Dr. Dave Williams rides the Canadarm to install a new piece of equipment on the ISS.

Dextre takes a break after finishing a task.

A Helping Hand

Not all space robots look like they just stepped out of a sci-fi movie. The Canadian-built robotic arm for the space shuttle is known as the Canadarm. And then there's Dextre, or Special Purpose Dexterous Manipulator (SPDM), a robot at the end of the Canadarm with hands that work like the various parts of a pocket-knife, making it possible to install, fix, and move equipment, and conduct experiments.

On my second spaceflight, I rode on the end of the Canadarm installing a piece of equipment on the outside of the ISS.

An Astronaut's Tool Kit

Not every machine in space is as high-tech as a robot. A basic drill can fix part of the robotic arm, or a shovel can help when you're collecting planetary rocks. But hold on tight if you don't want your tools floating away. Speaking of floating . . . your best tool on a space walk might be your safety tethers!

Rock Re-Entry

One of the simplest tools in space is a box. It was a box, after all, that carried Moon rocks back to Earth. Usually, these boxes have fancy names—like Special Environmental Sample Container—and they come with a seal to make sure the sample inside is protected. You wouldn't want to break the Mars rocks on the way back to Earth, would you?

NASA officials hold a box carrying the first Moon rocks from the *Apollo 11* mission in 1969.

Progress Payload

Astronauts are always fixing and maintaining equipment. A variety of tools are kept in modules throughout the spacecraft so the astronauts will have what they need when it's time to make a repair. But space on the ISS is limited, so spacecraft like the *Progress* resupply ship are used to get items to space: not just tools, but food, water, and materials for science experiments. Once the ship has unloaded, it's filled with waste and dirty clothes and sent back to Earth.

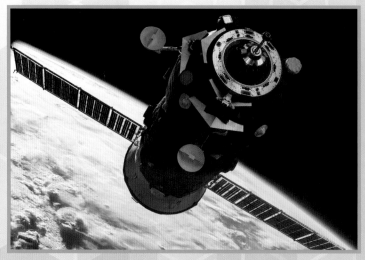

Progress approaches the ISS for docking.

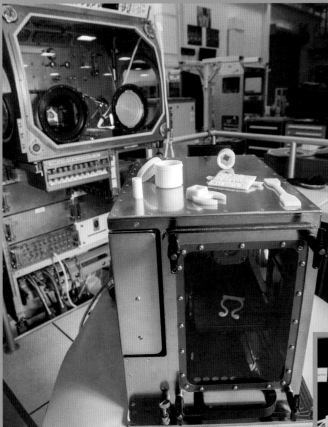

The Made In Space 3-D printer

Planetary Printer

What if you need something in space and the next resupply ship isn't due for a few months? Luckily, 3-D printers can make objects—even in space. A 3-D printer is not actually a printer; it's a manufacturing machine that makes a three-dimensional object out of a two-dimensional design. The ISS's 3-D printer has manufactured a wrench and an espresso coffee cup!

With a 3-D printer, a variety of tools can be manufactured aboard the ISS.

Here, Rover!

For astronauts, planetary exploration means heading outside the habitat. But you can only space walk so far in a bulky space suit. To really get around, you need a rover.

1000 ... giant... *gasp* ...steps ...for... *pant* ...humankind

The rover's tire treads are made of titanium to provide traction.

Astronaut Gene Cernan rides the *Apollo 17* Lunar Roving Vehicle.

Moon Buggy, Dune Buggy

The lunar rover that the Apollo astronauts used to explore the Moon looked like a dune buggy. Before landing, this very small vehicle was folded up in the spacecraft. Once the mission touched down, the rover was unfolded and put together by the astronauts. The battery-powered front and back motors gave the vehicle a top speed of 13 kilometers (8 miles) an hour, but on the Moon, where there is much less gravity than on Earth, astronauts zipped around at speeds up to 18 kilometers (11 miles) an hour.

Curious about Mars

Curiosity touched down on Mars on August 4, 2012. This exploratory rover is the size of a small car, but it comes with some pretty high-tech features, including 17 cameras, lasers that can vaporize anything that comes within 7 meters (23 feet), and a built-in nuclear power plant that can generate electricity for up to 14 years! It's busy taking rock samples and pictures so we can learn more about the history of the red planet.

The *Curiosity* rover

Mars 2020

The *Mars 2020* rover is set to launch in—you guessed it—2020. Its mission? To investigate a part of the planet that may have once supported life. *Mars 2020* will collect rock and soil samples and store them on the planet. If astronauts get there one day, they can bring the rocks home to study.

Bzzzzz

A concept drawing for *Mars 2020*

Suit Up!

When an astronaut needs to actually walk on a planet, a space suit is a must-have. More than just an awesome white outfit that proves you're an astronaut, a space suit is actually a human-sized spacecraft.

Power Walker

Space suits come with everything an astronaut needs to survive in the vacuum outside of the spacecraft or habitat where there is no air, including a life-support system (to supply oxygen and remove carbon dioxide) and a thermal-control system (to keep the temperature just right). The space suit has enough electrical power and batteries to last for a seven-hour walk. Batteries also power all these amazing systems and tools that help an astronaut conduct experiments and perform tasks:

* microphone (to speak to mission control)
* helmet (including a visor lined with gold to protect the eyes from the sun's harmful rays)
* protective layer (to prevent punctures in the suit)
* safety tether (to attach the suit to the ISS)
* gloves (to protect hands as they work)
* 35 mm camera (to take selfies!)
* color television camera ("Coming to you live from the Moon . . .")
* tool tether (so your wrench doesn't float away)

Astronaut Andrew Feustel suited up for a space walk outside the ISS

Space-walking isn't all science and exploration. In 1971, U.S. astronaut Alan Shepard of *Apollo 14* carried two golf balls with his equipment. He became the first human to play golf on the Moon.

Better SAFER Than Sorry

For space walks outside the ISS, zero-gravity suits feature a very cool mini-machine on the back. It's called a SAFER, which is short for Simplified Aid for EVA Rescue. (EVA means Extravehicular Activity.) It looks like a jet pack and has a small set of controls that fits on the front of the suit. In case of an emergency during an EVA, an astronaut can fire up the unit's thrusters and get back to safety.

Astronaut wears the SAFER jets on the corner of a PLSS (personalized life support system) backpack

Goodbye, Galaxy

Once an astronaut's work is done and a mission is complete, it's time to head back to Earth. So, how do spacecraft make it home?

Twice As Nice

Spacecraft designed to return to Earth need a rocket that can fire twice. The first time, the goal of the rockets is to liftoff and speed up the spacecraft so it can push through the atmosphere and get into orbit. The second time, the rockets are used to slow it down for re-entry.

Put on the Brakes!

A spacecraft coming back to Earth uses retro-rockets to slow down and re-enter the atmosphere. Firing the rockets at the right time and getting the right entry angle into the atmosphere are critical. If the angle is too shallow, the spacecraft could land in the wrong place or stay in orbit; too steep, and the spacecraft could break up or burn up.

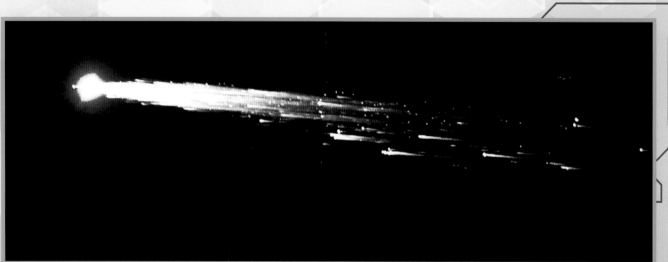

The *Jules Verne* ATV, an unmanned supply spacecraft, breaks up during re-entry into Earth's atmosphere.

When it was preparing to re-enter Earth's atmosphere, the space shuttle turned around backward so its engines pointed in the direction it was heading. This helped it to slow down for re-entry. Then it turned around again to enter the atmosphere.

On the Space Shuttle *Atlantis*, astronaut Lee Archambault prepares for re-entry.

Help from the Heat Shield

If you think the trickiest part of a mission is liftoff, think again! Coming home from space may actually be more dangerous than taking off. Why? Because traveling from the vacuum of space through the very dense air in the atmosphere causes a lot of friction. And friction causes heat! In fact, the temperature on the outside of the spacecraft can get as high as 1,600°C (2,912°F). Thanks to the amazing heat-shielding material on the outside of the spacecraft, the astronauts and equipment won't burn up on re-entry.

A heat shield being prepared for a mission to Mars

How Do We Land?

Re-entering Earth's atmosphere safely is hard enough, but you might need a few more devices—like parachutes and helicopters—to get an astronaut's feet on the ground.

From Space to Splashdown

"Splashdown" sounds like something you do at your community swimming pool, but it's actually a way of landing a spacecraft on water with the help of a parachute. The *Mercury*, *Gemini*, and *Apollo* capsules and today's *Dragon* capsule are capable of landing on water. These capsules fall back to Earth at supersonic speeds. Friction slows them down, but not enough. Once the capsule is close to Earth's surface, parachutes deploy and slow down the capsule even more, until it lands in the water. For early missions to space, NASA had a rescue ship waiting with a helicopter on board to pick up the astronauts and bring them home.

Divers recover the *Orion* spacecraft in the Pacific Ocean after splashdown.

A Bumpy Ride

The *Soyuz* capsule lands on the ground—in Kazakhstan, to be exact. The trip home from the ISS takes about three and a half hours and is made as comfortable as possible thanks to some amazing technology, including seat cushions specially designed to fit each astronaut's body. Astronauts are strapped in tight, but even with several landing rockets and four parachutes to slow the capsule down, everything and everyone inside get jostled around. Talk about motion sickness!

The *Soyuz* and its crew land safely with the help of a parachute.

Workers help astronauts exit the *Soyuz* after its landing in Kazakhstan.

Because there was no soft-landing system on his spacecraft, Yuri Gagarin had to eject himself out of his space capsule just 7 kilometers (4.3 miles) from the ground. With the help of two parachutes, he landed safely in a field.

41

Do You See What I See?

Telescope Talk

A telescope is an instrument used to make distant objects appear closer. Ever since Galileo Galilei pointed one to the sky in 1608 and spotted the Moon, human beings have been curious about our solar system and beyond. Today, telescopes on Earth and in space help us see what's out there so we can set our sights on future missions.

Data in the Dark

Some of the world's biggest space telescopes are found in remote areas where there are no distracting city lights.

* Gran Telescopio Canarias, on the Canary Islands, is the world's largest, at 10.4 meters (34 feet).
* ALMA (Atacama Large Millimeter Array), located in the Chilean desert, can see a golf ball 15 kilometers (9 miles) away.
* SALT (South African Large Telescope), about 400 kilometers (249 miles) from Cape Town, recently spotted a supermassive black hole.

The SALT inside its observatory

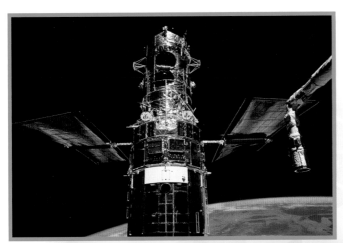

The Hubble in Space Shuttle *Endeavour*'s payload bay

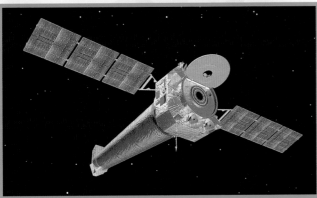

A computerized image of the Chandra X-ray Observatory in space

Orbital Observation

Telescopes can also orbit in outer space to observe distant planets and galaxies. Nearly the size of a school bus, the Hubble Space Telescope, which launched in 1990, sends pictures of our galaxy back to Earth and is powered by the sun. The Chandra X-ray Observatory, launched in 1999, detects X-ray emissions from exploded stars, black holes, and galaxy clusters.

Tomorrow's Telescope

The James Webb Space Telescope, launched in 2018, is the largest space observatory yet. Will it find another Earth-like planet that can sustain life?

* It's as big as a tennis court and 12 meters (40 feet) high. It had to be folded up for the trip into space and unfolded itself once there.
* It's going far—almost 1.5 million kilometers (932,000 miles) from Earth.
* It's got bling—the telescope's mirrors are coated in gold to help reflect ultra-red light from the universe's farthest objects.

Mirrors being tested before placement in the James Webb Space Telescope

Is That Star Moving?

At night, you may see airplanes and shooting stars when you look up, but if you see a bright object moving slowly and steadily across the sky, you're probably looking at a satellite—and you won't believe just how many jobs they have.

Satellite Savvy

A satellite is really just an object that orbits a planet. The Moon is a natural satellite around Earth, and planets, like Jupiter, can have moons, too. But there are also human-made, or artificial, satellites. In 1957, the Russian *Sputnik 1* was the first artificial satellite ever launched. Since then, thousands have been sent into space, including the ISS. Many scientific satellites, like telescopes and spacecraft, orbit around Earth, the Moon, Venus, Mars, and Jupiter, collecting information and sending it back to Earth.

A *Sputnik 1* replica at the National Air and Space Museum

A trio of small satellites after release from the International Space Station

This Spartan X-ray satellite was used to observe dust clouds in space.

Working Hard for Humans

Artificial satellites make our day-to-day lives easier. They allow us to send telephone calls, radio and TV programs, and computer data around the world. They help cars, airplanes, and ships figure out the best way to get where they are going. Want to know if you need an umbrella? Your local weather forecast relies on satellites, too. And, of course, scientific satellites like the Hubble telescope collect information about space and send it back to Earth.

A miniature Earth-observing satellite called a CubeSat is readied for launch.

Up and Down

How do satellites work? Although they are complicated machines featuring high-tech computer systems, they transmit information to us in three basic steps:

* Step 1: Uplink—Data is sent to the satellite from a station on Earth.
* Step 2: Reception—Data is received and processed on board the satellite.
* Step 3: Downlink—Data is sent back to another station somewhere else on Earth.

Free-Floating Future

Rockets, rovers, robots . . . all of these amazing machines are must-haves for missions to outer space. For future missions—where we go farther and stay longer—we will need to invent new devices and equipment that can keep humans safe on our quest.

Rocket Ride to Mars

NASA is working on a state-of-the-art rocket booster that will take us beyond Earth's orbit and into deep space. The Space Launch System, or SLS, is the world's most powerful rocket. It's designed to launch the brand-new *Orion* spacecraft to asteroids and, one day . . . to Mars!

Drones on the Moon

The idea of living on the Moon seems far-fetched, but engineers are designing drones to explore the Moon's extinct volcanoes. Why? To search for water and minerals that future citizens might use.

Testing an SLS model at NASA's Langley Research Center in Virginia

Superhero Systems!

Flying asteroids destroying Earth might seem like science fiction, but NASA and the European Space Agency are developing devices to change the path of Earth-bound asteroids by smashing them with a probe! Also in the works? A space shotgun capable of shooting falling space rocks.

At the FIRST robotics competition in Orlando, Florida, high-school inventors tinker with their design.

The Best "Machine" of All

We wouldn't have all of these super-cool, high-tech, state-of-the-art machines if it weren't for the most amazing machine of all: the human brain. Of course, your brain isn't *really* a machine, but without it, we can't invent, develop, and produce the equipment and technology that will help us on our journey to the next frontier. Like rocket fuel powers an engine, your cosmic curiosity fuels your brain. What mission machines will *your* brain help invent?

FURTHER READING

Eason, Sarah. *How Does a Rocket Work?* Gareth Stevens Publishing, 2010.

Graham, Ian. *Machines at Work In Space.* QEB Publishing, 2005.

Parker, Steve. *Machines Rule! In Space.* Franklin Watts, 2011.

Pfiffikus. *Think Like an Astronaut! How Do Rockets Work?* Pfiffikus, 2016.

Williams, Dave (Author), Cunti, Loredana (Author)and Krynauw, Theo (Illustrator). *To Burp or Not To Burp: A Guide to Your Body in Space.* Annick Press, 2016.

Williams, Dave (Author), Cunti, Loredana (Author) and Krynauw, Theo (Illustrator). *Go for Liftoff! How to Train Like an Astronaut.* Annick Press, 2017.

IMAGE CREDITS

INDEX

Cover art/design by Theo Krynauw/Sheryl Shapiro
Edited by Linda Pruessen
Designed by Sheryl Shapiro

We acknowledge the support of the Canada Council for the Arts, the Ontario Arts Council, and the participation of the Government of Canada/la participation du gouvernement du Canada for our publishing activities.

Funded by the Government of Canada   Financé par le gouvernement du Canada

Canada

ONTARIO ARTS COUNCIL
CONSEIL DES ARTS DE L'ONTARIO
an Ontario government agency
un organisme du gouvernement de l'Ontario

Cataloging in Publication

Williams, Dafydd, 1954-, author
Mighty mission machines : from rockets to rovers /
Dr. Dave Williams and Loredana Cunti ; Theo Krynauw, illustrator.

(Dr. Dave, astronaut)
Issued in print and electronic formats.
ISBN 978-1-77321-013-1 (hardcover).—ISBN 978-1-77321-012-4 (softcover).—
ISBN 978-1-77321-015-5 (PDF).—ISBN 978-1-77321-014-8 (EPUB)
1. Space vehicles—Juvenile literature. 2. Space vehicles—Design and
construction—Juvenile literature. I. Cunti, Loredana, 1968-, author
II. Krynauw, Theo, illustrator III. Title. IV. Series: Williams, Dafydd,
1954- . Dr. Dave, astronaut.

TL795.W55 2017   j629.47   C2017-905808-8
C2017-905809-6

Distributed in Canada by University of Toronto Press.
Published in the U.S.A. by Annick Press (U.S.) Ltd.
Distributed in the U.S.A. by Publishers Group West.

Printed in China

Visit us at: www.annickpress.com

Also available in e-book format. Please visit www.annickpress.com/ebooks.html for more details.

To all readers, may this book stimulate your curiosity to imagine and build the next generation of mighty machines that will help us explore farther, stay longer, and learn more about our solar system, our planet, and the future of human space exploration. —D.W.

To my brothers John and Claudio, for sharing with me their love of things that go fast. —L.C.